Skunks

Victoria Blakemore

© 2018 Victoria Blakemore

All rights reserved. This book or parts thereof may not be reproduced in any form, stored in any retrieval system, or transmitted in any form by any means—electronic, mechanical, photocopy, recording, or otherwise—without prior written permission of the publisher, except as provided by United States of America copyright law. For permission requests, write to the publisher, at "Attention: Permissions Coordinator," at the address below.

vblakemore.author@gmail.com

Copyright info/picture credits

Cover, Geoffrey Kuchera/Shutterstock; Page 3, Michael Meijer/AdobeStock; Page 5, skeeze/Pixabay; Page 7, skeeze/Pixabay; Page 9, Pomaikai/Fotolia; Pages 10-11, geraldfriedrich2/Pixabay; Page 13, Yasmins World/Shutterstock; Page 15, Geoffrey Kuchera/Shutterstock; Page 17, Eudyptula/AdobeStock; Page 19, ASP Inc/AdobeStock; Page 21, gnagel/AdobeStock; Page 23; Adwo/AdobeStock; Page 25, Heiko Kiera/Shutterstock; Page 27, Cynthia Kidwell/Shutterstock; Page 29, Bob Azzaro/Shutterstock; Page 31, sunsinger/AdobeStock; Page 33, Geoffrey Kuchera/Shutterstock

Table of Contents

What are Skunks?	2
Size	4
Physical Characteristics	6
Habitat	8
Range	10
Diet	12
Communication	16
Movement	18
Skunk Kits	20
Skunk Life	22
Self Defense	24
Population	26
Skunks as Pets	28
Helping Skunks	30
Glossary	34

What Are Skunks?

Skunks are small mammals that are known for their strong smell. They are related to an animal called the stink badger.

There are eleven different kinds of skunks. They differ in color, size, markings, and where they live.

Most skunks are black and white, but some are cream and brown.

Size

Skunks are usually about the size of a cat. Most can grow to be about nineteen inches long. Their tail can grow to be fifteen inches long.

The eastern hog-nosed skunk is the largest skunk. It can be nearly three feet long.

Skunks usually weigh between six and ten pounds.

Physical Characteristics

Skunks have sharp claws. Their claws are used to help them dig up insects and grubs to eat.

They have a long snout, which can help them to find food. It can also help them to smell predators that may be nearby.

The striped skunk is known for the white stripes that is has along its back. Each striped skunk has a slightly different stripe.

Habitat

Skunks are often found in woodlands and the mountains. They can also be found in the desert.

In areas where it is cold, skunks sleep for much of the winter. In warmer **climates**, they do not need to sleep during the winter.

Range

Almost all skunks live in North America, but there are some that are found in Asia.

Skunks are commonly seen in parts of Canada, Mexico, and the United States.

Diet

Skunks are **omnivores**, which means that they eat meat and plants.

Their diet is made up of insects, fruit, nuts, plants, and small mammals. They use their long, sharp claws to dig up insects and grubs to eat.

Skunks do not have very good eyesight. They usually use their sense of smell to find food.

Skunks are often thought to be pests. Their smell is the main reason. They can also cause damage to yards when they are digging for food.

Skunks have also been known to carry **rabies**. They can make people or animals very sick if they bite them.

Skunks can get into trash cans if they smell something good. They can make a big mess.

Communication

Skunks usually use sound and movement to communicate with each other.

They are usually very quiet animals, but can make a few different sounds. They can hiss, growl, screech, and make a cooing sound.

They often use movements like stamping their feet as a warning to other animals.

Movement

Skunks usually move slowly because they do not see very well. They can run up to ten miles per hour for short distances if needed.

They are able to swim, but they are not often seen in the water.

Skunks are not very good at climbing. They are rarely seen very high off the ground.

Skunk Kits

Skunks usually have a **litter** of about six babies. Their babies are called kits.

The kits are born blind, with no fur. They are able to spray their oil before they can see. Mother skunks protect their kits from predators.

Young skunks will stay with their mother for about a year. Then, they go out on their own.

Skunk Life

Skunks live in burrows that they dig in the ground. They may also make their burrow in hollowed out logs or in holes abandoned by other animals.

They are usually **solitary**, which means that they spend most of their time alone.

They are **nocturnal**. They usually rest during the day and are most active at night.

Self Defense

Skunks have a special scent gland under their tail that makes a strong smelling oil. Skunks spray this oil when predators get too close.

They usually give the predator a warning, by stomping the ground and growling.

If the predator doesn't leave, skunks lift their tail and spray. The oil has a very strong smell and is very hard to get rid of.

Population

Skunks are not **endangered**. All skunk populations are **stable** except for one. The pygmy spotted skunk is **vulnerable** due to **declining** population.

Skunks are able to **adapt** to living in different habitats. This has allowed many skunk populations to be **stable**.

In the wild, skunks can live up to ten years. However, they usually live less than six years.

Skunks as Pets

Some skunks are **domesticated**. They are used to being around humans. Some people even keep skunks as pets.

Pet skunks have been **de-scented**. They do not make the stinky oil that skunks are known for.

People who have pet skunks say they are very playful and loving animals.

Helping Skunks

Pollution, habitat loss, disease, and **overpopulation** can all be problems for skunks.

Some places have hunting seasons when skunks can be hunted. This helps to keep the population from growing too large for the habitat to support.

Many groups focus on taking care of the environment. They clean up polluted habitats and educate people about ways to help the environment.

Some people keep skunks from being pests by fencing in their yards. This can prevent problems between skunks and people.

Glossary

Adapt: to change or adjust

Climate: the usual weather in a particular place

Declining: getting smaller

De-scented: when a skunk's scent glands are removed so they do not make their smelly oil

Domesticated: animals that are used to living with humans, not in the wild

Endangered: at risk of becoming extinct

Litter: a group of animals that are born at the same time

Nocturnal: animals that are active at night

Omnivore: animals that eat meat and plants

Overpopulation: when there are too many of an animal for the habitat to support

Rabies: a dangerous virus that wild animals can spread to other animals or humans

Solitary: living alone

Stable: steady, unchanging

Vulnerable: when an animal may become threatened or endangered because of declining population

About the Author

Victoria Blakemore is a first grade teacher in Southwest Florida with a passion for reading.

You can visit her at

www.elementaryexplorers.com

Also in This Series

Also in This Series

www.ingramcontent.com/pod-product-compliance
Lightning Source LLC
Chambersburg PA
CBHW040221040426
42333CB00049B/3198